Maths made Merry

Workbook Grade 4

Om KIDZ
An imprint of Om Books International

NUMBER MAZE

Fill up the maze with the correct numbers to help Aster the Astrogirl reach the Earth.

SUCCESSORS IN SPACE

Look at the numbers on the stars and write their successors in the boxes below them.

1241

5253

9990

3999

7898

4578

3616

4217

PLANETARY PREDECESSORS

Match the numbers on the planets to their predecessors on the spaceships.

MISSING NUMBERS

Fill in the missing numbers on the starry paths below.

1234 1236 1238

4500 4510 4515

3124 3129 3144 3149

4113 4119 4127

SPACE SIGNS

Read the space problems and fill the correct sign in the boxes.

Arnie the Alien made 1498 spaceships. Argo the Alien made 1948. Who has more spaceships?

Arnie ☐ **Argo**

Andy Astroboy spotted 4614 asteroids in space. Allie Astrogirl spotted 4164. Who spotted less asteroids?

Andy ☐ **Allie**

Martians visited Earth and bought 3969 candies. Venusians visited Earth and bought 3696 candies. Who bought more?

Martians ☐ **Venusians**

The moon had 909 visitors this year. It had 990 visitors last year. Which year had lesser visitors?

This year ☐ **Last year**

ROMAN NUMBERS

Help the aliens match the Roman Numbers to the correct rocket.

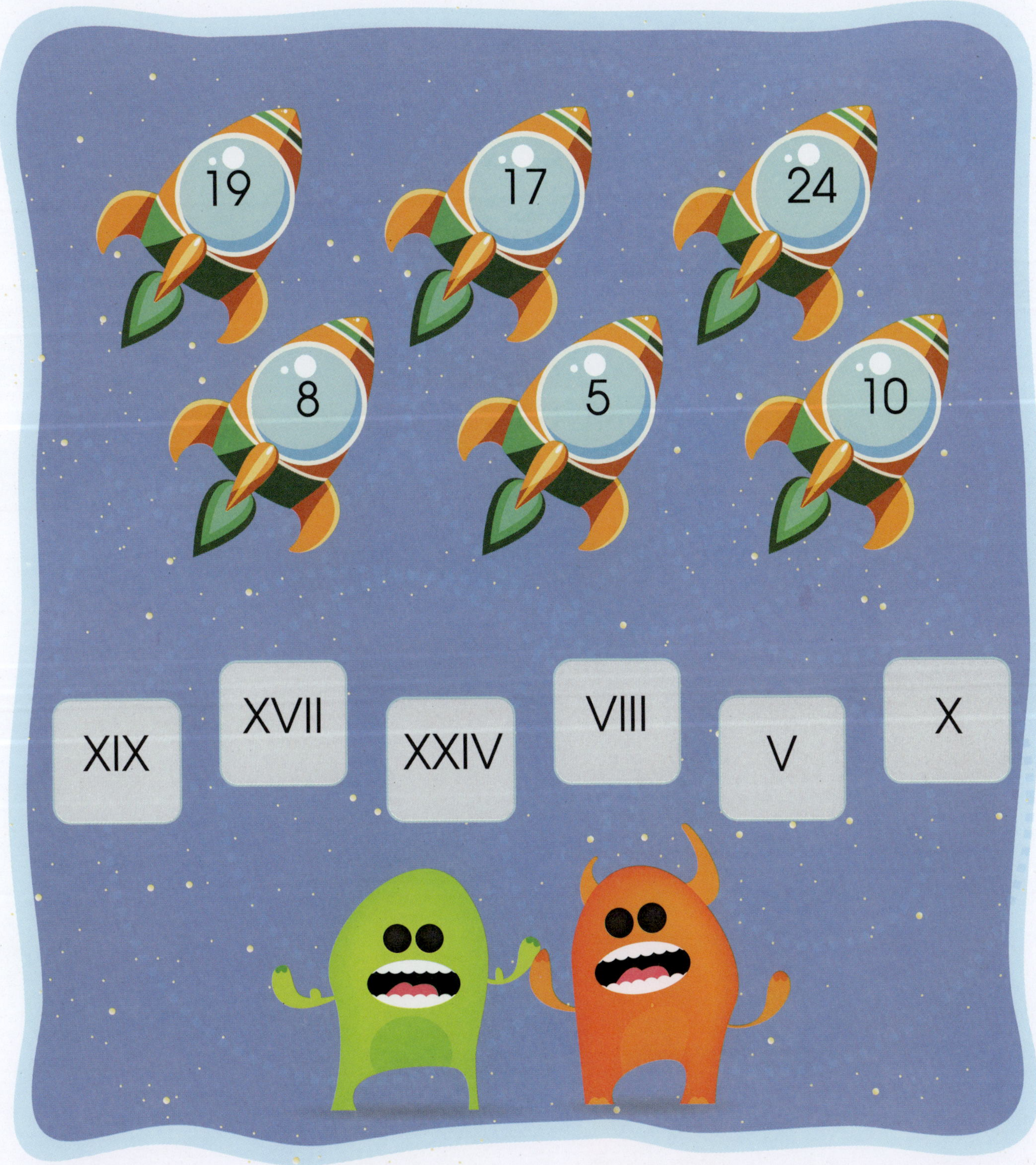

MARTIAN MATH

Help the Martians solve the sums on the planets below.

```
  110
+ 90
+ 12
```

```
  707
+ 522
```

```
  541
+ 80
+ 40
```

```
  216
+ 100
+ 111
```

```
   406
+  300
+  230
+ 1036
```

555
+ 111
+ 222

435
+ 825
+ 614

258
+ 14
+ 517

184
+ 217
+ 312

228
+ 262
+ 301

ALIEN ADDITION

Help these aliens fill in the blanks with the correct numbers to solve their addition problems.

1473 + 2139 = ______

5065 + 3459 = ______

7608 + 1562 = ______

3917 + 931 = ______

4926 + 1784 = ______

7020 + 2451 = ______

1589 + 5419

1363 + 1973

1033 + 162

2915 + 3171

2431 + 102

1825 + 1221

PLANET PROBLEMS

Solve the sums on the planets below.

$$\begin{array}{r} 216 \\ -\ 74 \\ \hline \end{array}$$

$$\begin{array}{r} 210 \\ -\ 34 \\ \hline \end{array}$$

$$\begin{array}{r} 465 \\ -\ 432 \\ \hline \end{array}$$

$$\begin{array}{r} 539 \\ -\ 26 \\ \hline \end{array}$$

$$\begin{array}{r} 923 \\ -\ 152 \\ \hline \end{array}$$

$$\begin{array}{r} 818 \\ -\ 428 \\ \hline \end{array}$$

$$\begin{array}{r} 517 \\ -\,143 \\ \hline \end{array}$$

$$\begin{array}{r} 856 \\ -\,811 \\ \hline \end{array}$$

$$\begin{array}{r} 943 \\ -\,356 \\ \hline \end{array}$$

$$\begin{array}{r} 757 \\ -\,461 \\ \hline \end{array}$$

$$\begin{array}{r} 943 \\ -\,650 \\ \hline \end{array}$$

$$\begin{array}{r} 884 \\ -\,339 \\ \hline \end{array}$$

SUBTRACTING IN SPACE

Crack the codes put up by these space invaders to stop them from destroying our planet.

Take away 6354 from 8014

Take away 5679 from 6790

Take away 1935 from 6210

Take away 7667 from 8220

Take away 3482 from 7040

Take away 8411 from 9900

Take away 3209 from 5815

Take away 2428 from 2553

TOXO'S TABLES

Help Toxo the Alien learn multiplication tables by filling in the boxes below.

7		8		9	
7 × 1 =		8 × 1 =		9 × 1 =	
7 × 2 =		8 × 2 =		9 × 2 =	
7 × 3 =		8 × 3 =		9 × 3 =	
7 × 4 =		8 × 4 =		9 × 4 =	
7 × 5 =		8 × 5 =		9 × 5 =	
7 × 6 =		8 × 6 =		9 × 6 =	
7 × 7 =		8 × 7 =		9 × 7 =	
7 × 8 =		8 × 8 =		9 × 8 =	
7 × 9 =		8 × 9 =		9 × 9 =	
7 × 10 =		8 × 10 =		9 × 10 =	

10		11		12	
10 × 1 =		11 x 1 =		12 x 1 =	
10 × 2 =		11 × 2 =		12 × 2 =	
10 × 3 =		11 × 3 =		12 × 3 =	
10 × 4 =		11 × 4 =		12 × 4 =	
10 × 5 =		11 × 5 =		12 × 5 =	
10 × 6 =		11 × 6 =		12 × 6 =	
10 × 7 =		11 × 7 =		12 × 7 =	
10 × 8 =		11 × 8 =		12 × 8 =	
10 × 9 =		11 × 9 =		12 × 9 =	
10 × 10 =		11 × 10 =		12 × 10 =	

MULTIMANIA

Solve the sums on the UFOs below.

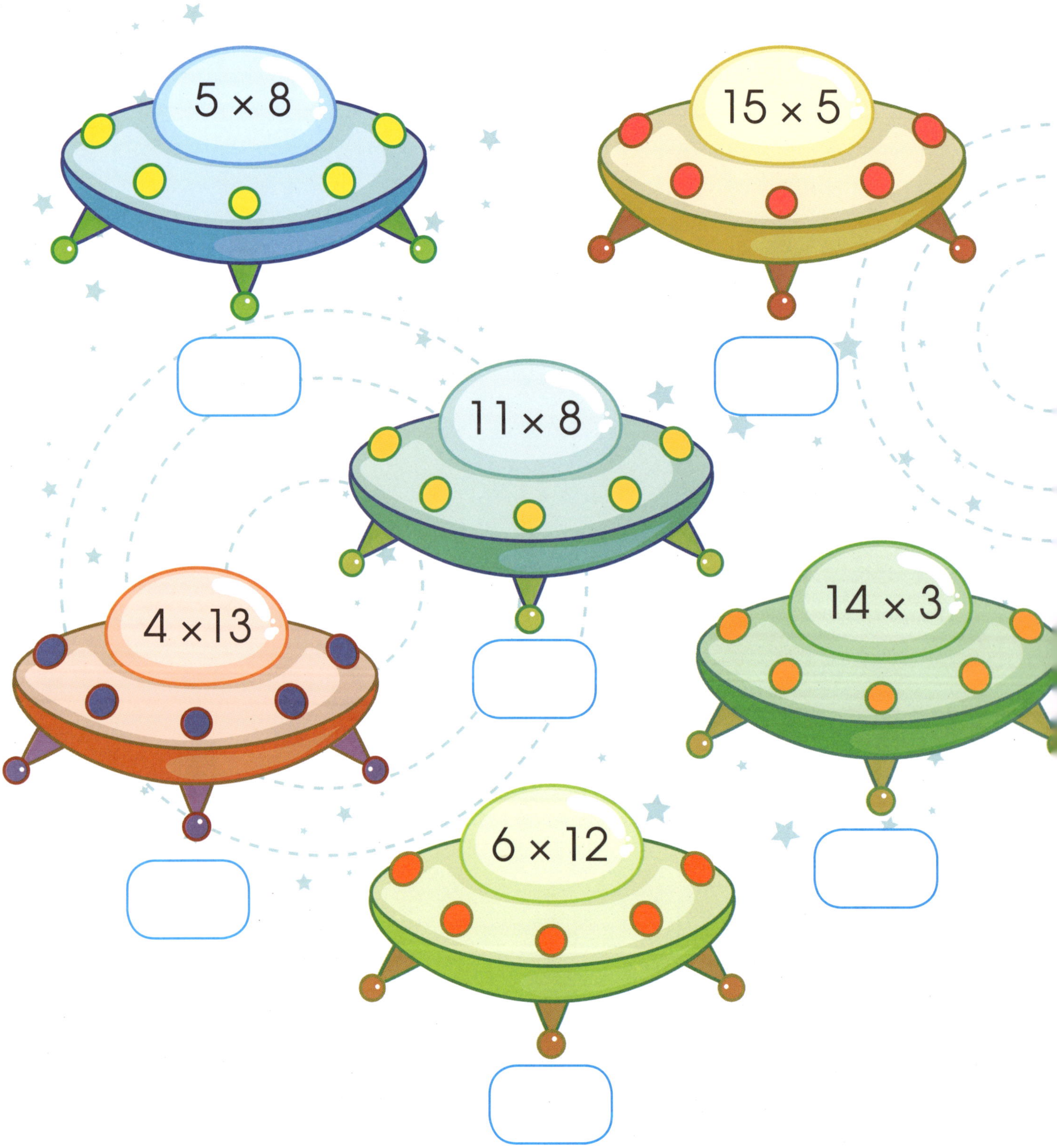

9×10 = ☐

8×8 = ☐

11×4 = ☐

6×5 = ☐

3×6 = ☐

7×9 = ☐

STARRY DIVIDE

Divide the sums on the stars below.

72 ÷ 18

Q ☐ ☐ R

42 ÷ 15

Q ☐ ☐ R

112 ÷ 12

Q ☐ ☐ R

42 ÷ 21

Q ☐ ☐ R

40 ÷ 15

Q ☐ ☐ R

39 ÷ 18

Q ☐ ☐ R

20 ÷ 16

Q ☐ ☐ R

81 ÷ 24

Q ☐ ☐ R

63 ÷ 14

Q ☐ ☐ R

48 ÷ 13

Q ☐ ☐ R

DIVIDE AND FILL

Fill in the blanks to complete the divisions on the spaceships below.

30 ÷ ______ = 6

______ ÷ 8 = 4

90 ÷ ______ = 10

30 ÷ ______ = 3

45 ÷ ______ = 9

______ ÷ 5 = 3

$12 \div \square = 6$

$\square \div 2 = 7$

$81 \div \square = 9$

$\square \div 5 = 1$

$40 \div \square = 8$

$\square \div 8 = 8$

MONSTER MATH

Help the aliens pass their math test by solving the sums below.

$(12 + 6) - 18$	
$18 - (8 - 5)$	
$7 + (4 - 2)$	
$10 + (11 - 10)$	
$14 + (20 + 12)$	
$16 - (3 + 1)$	

FRACTION FUN

Help Adam the Astroboy solve the fractions below.

$$\frac{9}{11} + \frac{3}{11} =$$

$$\frac{6}{10} + \frac{6}{10} =$$

$$\frac{5}{8} + \frac{1}{8} =$$

$$\frac{2}{12} + \frac{1}{12} =$$

$$\frac{2}{11} + \frac{3}{11} =$$

$$\frac{1}{6} + \frac{1}{6} =$$

LET'S MEASURE

Convert the measurements and help these aliens learn about them!

200 cm = ______ m

3 m = ______ cm

8 km = ______ m

1000 m = ______ km

80 mm = ______ cm

20 mm = ______ cm

AREAS AND ALIENS

These aliens are learning about areas. Can you help them?

This rectangle has a side of 5 cm and a perimeter of 22 cm. What is the length of the other side?

The sides of this square are 2 cm each. What is its area?

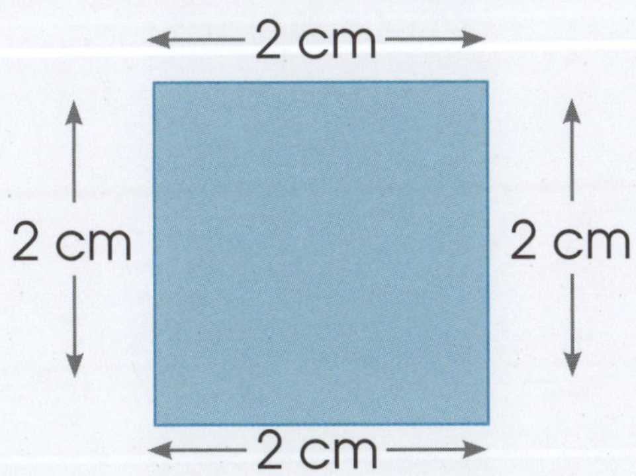

The sides of this square are 9 cm each. What is its area?

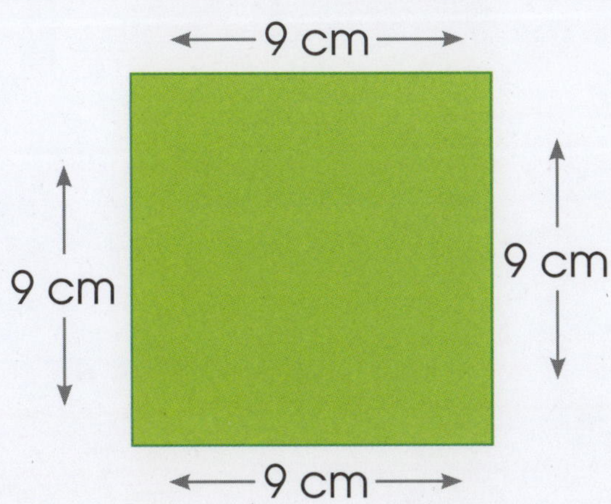

TICK TOCK

What does the clock say? Help these aliens tell the time.

ALL ABOUT MONEY

Help the aliens count how much money each of them have.

ALIEN GRAPH

These aliens held a popularity contest. Look at the graph to see how much each one scored. Then, fill in the blanks with the correct answers.

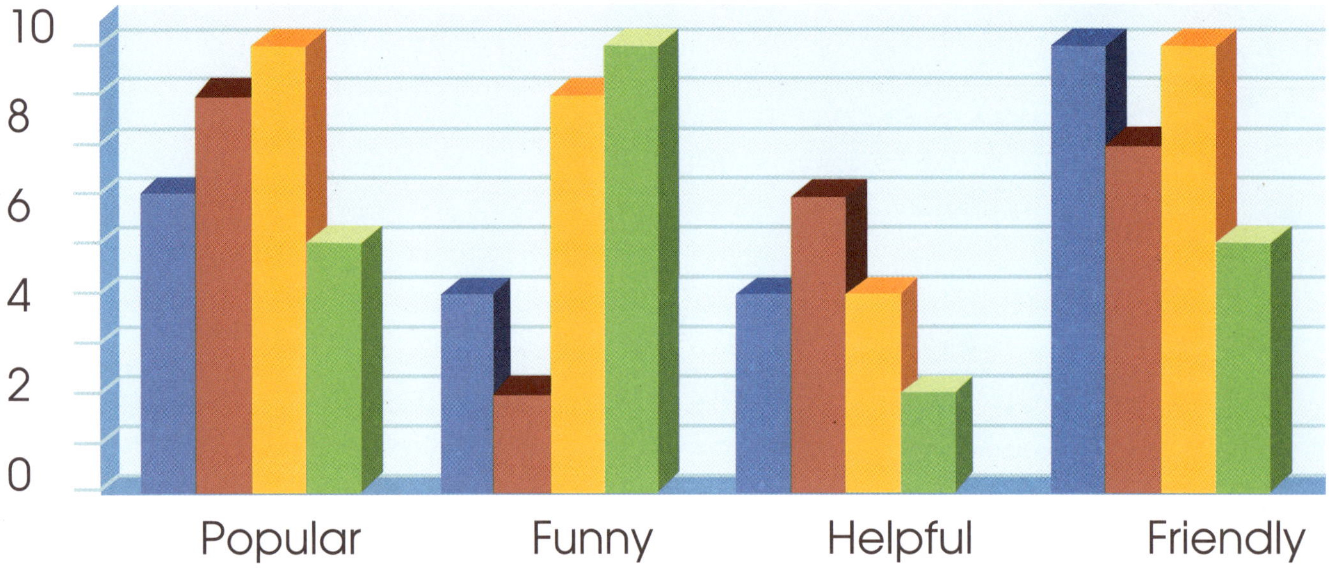

Which alien is the funniest?

____

Which alien is the most popular one?

____

Which alien is the least helpful one?

____

Which alien scores the highest overall?

____

ANSWERS

Page 2

1111, 1112, 1113, 1114, 1115, 1116, 1117, 1118, 1119, 1120, 1121, 1122, 1123, 1124, 1125, 1126, 1127, 1128, 1129, 1130, 1131, 1132, 1133, 1134, 1135, 1136, 1137, 1138, 1139, 1140

Page 3

Star	Answer
1241	1242
5253	5254
9990	9991
3999	4000
7898	7899
4578	4579
3616	3617
4217	4218

Page 4

Planet	Spaceship
7623	7622
1347	1346
2344	2343
8930	8929
5697	5696
3900	3899

Page 5

1234, 1236, 1238, **1240**, 1242, **1244**

4500, **4505**, 4510, 4515, **4520**, **4525**

3124, 3129, **3134**, **3139**, 3144, 3149

4113, **4116**, 4119, **4122**, **4125**, 4127

Page 6

Arnie the Alien made 1498 spaceships. Argo the Alien made 1948. Who has more spaceships?

Arnie < Argo

Andy Astroboy spotted 4614 asteroids in space. Allie Astrogirl spotted 4164. Who spotted less asteroids?

Andy > Allie

Martians visited Earth and bought 3969 candies. Venusians visited Earth and bought 3696 candies. Who bought more?

Martians > Venusians

The moon had 909 visitors this year. It had 990 visitors last year. Which year had lesser visitors?

This year < Last year

Page 7

19	XIX
17	XVII
24	XXIV
8	VIII
5	V
10	X

Page 8

110 + 90 + 12 = **212**

707 + 522 = **1229**

541 + 80 + 40 = **661**

216 + 100 + 111 = **427**

406 + 300 + 230 + 1036 = **1972**

Page 9

555 + 111 + 222 = **888**

435 + 825 + 614 = **1874**

258 + 14 + 517 = **789**

184 + 217 + 312 = **713**

228 + 262 + 301 = **791**

Page 10

1473 + 2139 = **3612**

5065 + 3459 = **8524**

7608 + 1562 = **9170**

3917 + 931 = **4848**

4926 + 1784 = **6710**

7020 + 2451 = **9471**

Page 11

1589 + 5419 = **7008**

1363 + 1973 = **3336**

1033 + 162 = **1195**

2915 + 3171 = **6086**

2431 + 102 = **2533**

1825 + 1221 = **3046**

Page 12

210 − 34 = **176**

216 − 74 = **142**

465 − 432 = **33**

539 − 26 = **513**

923 − 152 = **771**

818 − 428 = **390**

Page 13

517 − 143 = **374**

856 − 811 = **45**

943 − 356 = **587**

757 − 461 = **296**

943 − 650 = **293**

884 − 339 = **545**

Page 14

Take away 6354 from 8014 — 1660

Take away 5679 from 6790 — 1111

Take away 1935 from 6210 — 4275

Take away 7667 from 8220 — 553

Page 15

Take away 3482 from 7040 — 3558

Take away 8411 from 9900 — 1489

Take away 3209 from 5815 — 2606

Take away 2428 from 2553 — 125

Page 16

7		8		9	
7 × 1 =	7	8 × 1 =	8	9 × 1 =	9
7 × 2 =	14	8 × 2 =	16	9 × 2 =	18
7 × 3 =	21	8 × 3 =	24	9 × 3 =	27
7 × 4 =	28	8 × 4 =	32	9 × 4 =	36
7 × 5 =	35	8 × 5 =	40	9 × 5 =	45
7 × 6 =	42	8 × 6 =	48	9 × 6 =	54
7 × 7 =	49	8 × 7 =	56	9 × 7 =	63
7 × 8 =	56	8 × 8 =	64	9 × 8 =	72
7 × 9 =	63	8 × 9 =	72	9 × 9 =	81
7 × 10 =	70	8 × 10 =	80	9 × 10 =	90

Page 17

10		11		12	
10 × 1 =	10	11 × 1 =	11	12 × 1 =	12
10 × 2 =	20	11 × 2 =	22	12 × 2 =	24
10 × 3 =	30	11 × 3 =	33	12 × 3 =	36
10 × 4 =	40	11 × 4 =	44	12 × 4 =	48
10 × 5 =	50	11 × 5 =	55	12 × 5 =	60
10 × 6 =	60	11 × 6 =	66	12 × 6 =	72
10 × 7 =	70	11 × 7 =	77	12 × 7 =	84
10 × 8 =	80	11 × 8 =	88	12 × 8 =	96
10 × 9 =	90	11 × 9 =	99	12 × 9 =	108
10 × 10 =	100	11 × 10 =	110	12 × 10 =	120

ANSWERS

Page 18

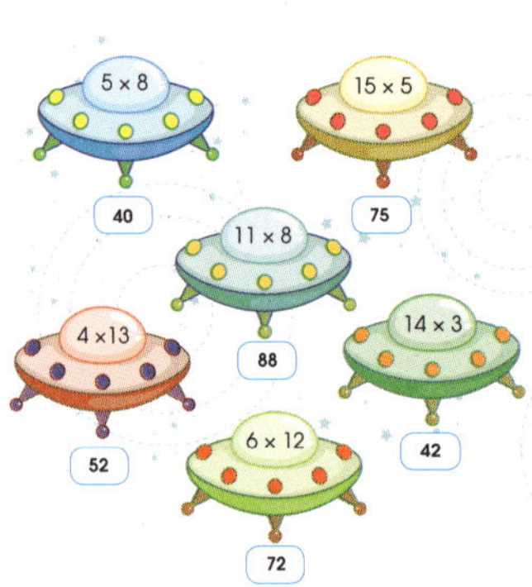

Page 19

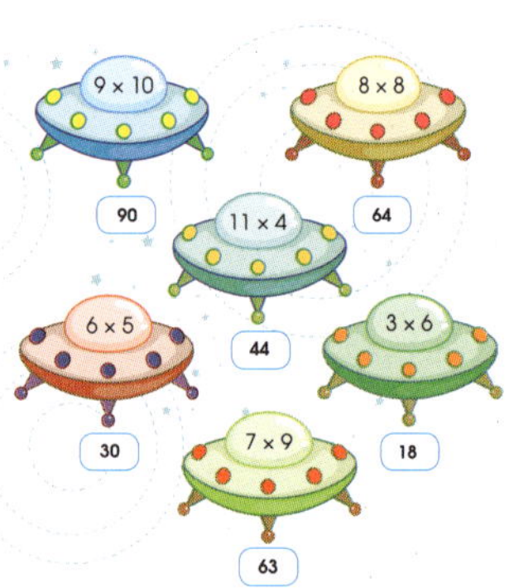

Page 20

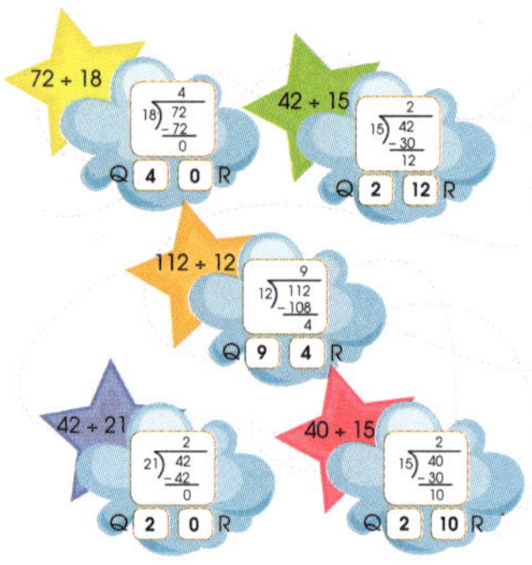

Page 21

Page 22

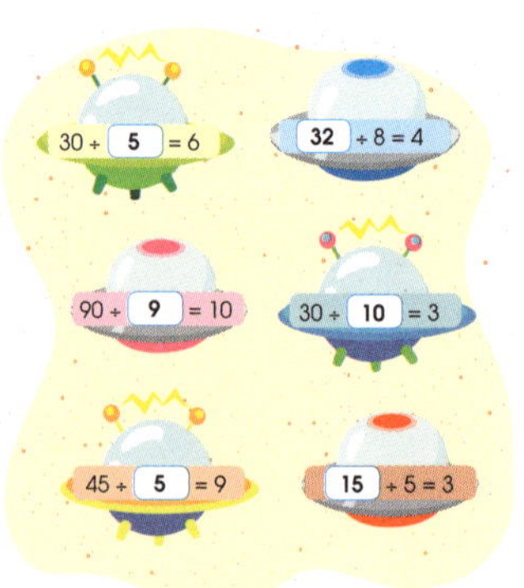

Page 23

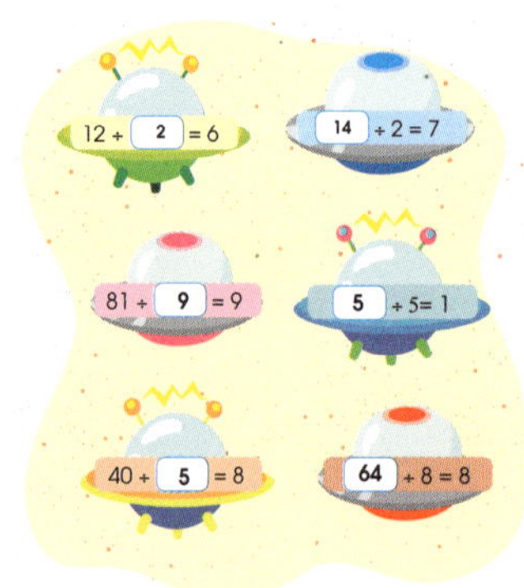

Page 24

(12 + 6) – 18	0
18 – (8 – 5)	15
7 + (4 – 2)	9
10 + (11 – 10)	11
14 + (20 + 12)	46
16 – (3 + 1)	12

Page 25

$\frac{9}{11} + \frac{3}{11} =$	$\frac{12}{11}$
$\frac{5}{8} + \frac{1}{8} =$	$\frac{6}{8}$
$\frac{2}{11} + \frac{3}{11} =$	$\frac{5}{11}$
$\frac{1}{6} + \frac{1}{6} =$	$\frac{2}{6}$
$\frac{6}{10} + \frac{6}{10} =$	$\frac{12}{10}$
$\frac{2}{12} + \frac{1}{12} =$	$\frac{3}{12}$

Page 26

200 cm =	2 m
3 m =	300 cm
8 km =	8000 m
1,000 m =	1 km
80 mm =	8 cm
20 mm =	2 cm

Page 27

This rectangle has a side of 5 cm and a perimeter of 22 cm. What is the length of the other side?

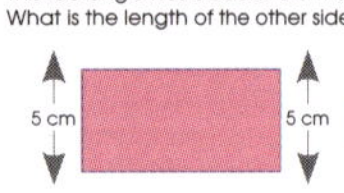

6 cm

The sides of this square are 2 cm each. What is its area?

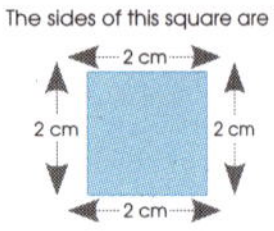

4 cm²

The sides of this square are 9 cm each. What is its area?

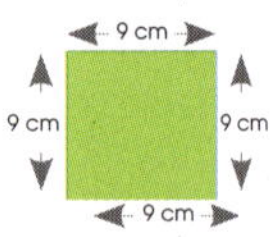

81 cm²

Page 28

Page 29

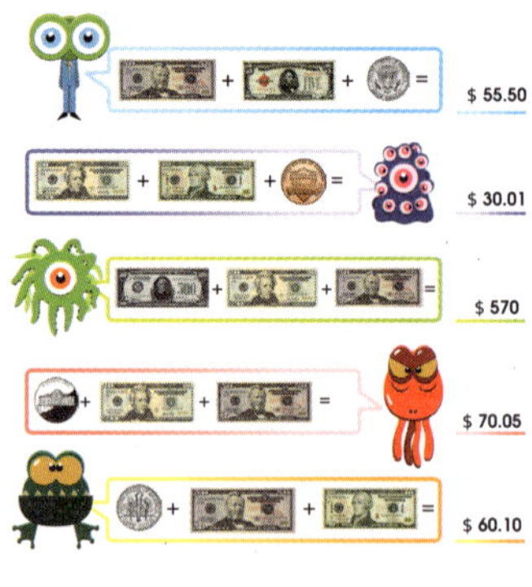

Page 30

Which alien is the funniest?
Alien 4

Which alien is the most popular one?
Alien 3

Which alien is the least helpful one?
Alien 4

Which alien scores the highest overall?
Alien 3